Bilingual Edition

READING POWER

Edición Bilingüe

Record-Breaking Animals

The Hummingbird
World's Smallest Bird

El colibrí
El pájaro más pequeño del mundo

Joy Paige

The Rosen Publishing Group's
PowerKids Press™ & Buenas Letras™
New York

1

Published in 2003 by The Rosen Publishing Group, Inc.
29 East 21st Street, New York, NY 10010

First Bilingual Edition 2003
First Edition in English 2002

Book Design: Michael DeLisio
Photo Credits: Cover © Mary Ann McDonald/Corbis; pp. 5, 12–13,
14–15, 17 © Joe McDonald/Corbis; pp. 7, 21 © George Lepp/Corbis;
pp. 9, 11, 19 © Animals Animals

Paige, Joy
The Hummingbird: World's smallest animal/El colibrí: El pájaro más
pequeño del mundo/Joy Paige ; traducción al español: Spanish Educational
Publishing
p. cm. — (Record-Breaking Animals)
Includes bibliographical references and index.
ISBN 0-8239-6894-4 (lib. bdg.)
1. Blue whale—Juvenile literature. [1. Blue whale. 2. Whales. 3. Spanish
Language Materials—Bilingual.] I. Title.

Printed in The United States of America

Contents

Contenido

This is a hummingbird.
A hummingbird is a
very small bird.

Este pájaro es un colibrí.
Es un pajarito muy pequeño.

5

Hummingbirds lay eggs
in a nest. The eggs are
very small.

Los colibríes ponen huevos
en un nido.
Los huevos son muy pequeños.

A hummingbird baby is tiny. This baby fits on a coin.

———————————

Los pichones de colibrí son diminutos.
Son más pequeños que una moneda.

9

Hummingbird wings go very fast. This helps them fly forward and backward.

Los colibríes mueven las alas muy rápido.
Así pueden volar hacia adelante y hacia atrás.

Hummingbird wings make a humming sound. This hum gives the birds their name.

Las alas de los colibríes hacen un zumbido al moverse.

12

Hummingbirds can stay
in one place when they fly.
They can hover.

———————————————

Los colibríes pueden quedarse
en un mismo lugar.
Parece que flotan en el aire.

Hummingbirds fly from
flower to flower to get
food. This food is
called nectar.

Los colibríes vuelan
de flor en flor
en busca de alimento.
Beben el néctar de las flores.

Hummingbirds have long beaks. Hummingbirds use their beaks to drink nectar from flowers.

Los colibríes tienen el pico muy largo.
Beben el néctar de las flores con el pico.

The hummingbird is smaller than most flowers. The hummingbird is the smallest bird in the world!

Los colibríes son más pequeños que la mayoría de las flores. ¡El colibrí es el pájaro más pequeño del mundo!

Glossary

backward (**bak**-wuhrd) opposite to the
usual way

beaks (**beeks**) birds' bills

hover (**huhv**-uhr) to stay in one place in the air

nectar (**nehk**-tuhr) a sweet liquid found in
many flowers

tiny (**ty**-nee) very small

Glosario

alimento (**el**) comida

diminuto(**a**) muy pequeñito

flotar quedar suspendido en el aire o en el agua

néctar (**el**) líquido dulce que se encuentra dentro de muchas
flores

pichones (**los**) crías de los pajaros

zumbido (**el**) ruido sordo

Resources / Recursos

Here are more books to read about hummingbirds:
Otros libros que puedes leer sobre el colibrí:

A Hummingbird's Life
by John Himmelman
Children's Press (2000)

Hummingbird
by Rebecca Stefoff
Marshall Cavendish, Inc. (1997)

Web sites
Due to the changing nature of Internet links, PowerKids Press has developed an online list of Web sites related to the subject of this book. This site is updated regularly. Please use this link to access the list:

Sitios web
Debido a las constantes modificaciones en los sitios de Internet, PowerKids Press ha desarrollado una guía on-line de sitios relacionados al tema de este libro. Nuestro sitio web se actualiza constantemente. Por favor utiliza la siguiente dirección para consultar la lista:

http://www.buenasletraslinks.com/chl/tmb

Word count in English: 113
Número de palabras en español: 126

Index

Índice